IF YOU LIE TO OTHERS,

YOU LIE TO YOURSELF.

2018 Catherine Fet
North Landing Books
all rights reserved

WHAT IS A LIE?

A lie is something we say to deceive others.
A lie is almost always intentional.
A person intends, or plans, to deceive others.
But it's also possible to make a mistake
that comes across as a lie.
Lies are always harmful except if they are
part of a game where lying is allowed.
There are different kinds of lies,
and different words
that describe lying.

Here are a few:

DISINFORMATION is giving wrong information about something

A COVER-UP is lying about something you did, for example, to hide a mistake you made

A FIB is a word used for a small lie. It's still bad, but it doesn't harm anyone. For example, if the teacher asks *Where is your homework?* and you say *My dog ate it*, it's a fib.

A HALF-TRUTH is when what a person says is only partly true

A FALSE PROMISE is promising something you know you won't do

WHAT IS A LIE? (2)

THERE ARE A FEW TYPES OF LIES THAT MANY PEOPLE BELIEVE ARE NOT HARMFUL:

EXAGGERATION IS WHEN YOU MAKE SOMETHING LOOK BIGGER THAN WHAT IT ACTUALLY IS TO IMPRESS A PERSON. FOR EXAMPLE, WHEN I SAY TO MY SON, *I TOLD YOU A MILLION TIMES NOT TO DO THAT!* IT'S AN EXAGGERATION, MAYBE I TOLD HIM ONLY 110 TIMES.

A BLUFF IS PRETENDING YOU CAN OR CAN'T DO SOMETHING IN A GAME TO TRICK OTHER PLAYERS INTO GIVING UP OR MAKING A MISTAKE. POKER IS A CARD GAME FAMOUS FOR BLUFFING.

A WHITE LIE IS WHEN A PERSON IS SAYING SOMETHING THAT IS UNTRUE IN ORDER TO PROTECT SOMEONE FROM BEING UPSET. FOR EXAMPLE, IF A PERSON WHO IS REALLY SICK ASKS A DOCTOR *WILL I BE OK?* AND THE DOCTOR SAYS *SURE*, IT MAY BE A WHITE LIE IF A DOCTOR IS NOT REALLY SURE, BUT DOESN'T WANT TO UPSET THE SICK PERSON.

Crossing Your Fingers

Some people - mostly kids - believe that if they say a lie or make a false promise while secretly crossing their fingers, the lie or the false promise doesn't count. For example, making a promise, like *I'll never do it again, I promise!* a person would cross their index and middle fingers in their pocket, under a table, or behind their back. They think this counts as not making any promise at all! Where did that idea come from?

It's possible that the gesture of crossed fingers has roots in Ancient Rome where it was dangerous to be a Christian, a follower of Jesus Christ. Romans killed Christians as enemies because they believed that Christianity didn't respect the authority of the Roman state. So Christians came up with a secret sign of crossed fingers - this is how they recognized each other. Over time, after the Roman Empire fell and Europe became Christian, people started to use crossed fingers to wish luck to each other, and also as a sign of magic protection from evil. Lying is evil, so at some point they also started crossing fingers when lying to protect themselves from the consequences of their own lie. Well, the truth is crossing your fingers never works: Lying gets you in trouble whether you cross your fingers or not!

Why People Lie

There are 4 main reasons people lie:

1. To avoid punishment
Lying often starts with wrong-doing or a mistake. Instead of admitting the mistake, a person denies it and points the finger at others. (*The dog ate my homework!*) Sometimes the person doesn't deny the wrong-doing, but comes up with a story to explain why they behaved this way. (*I am late because the clock broke!*)

2. To avoid embarrassmemt
Embarrassment is a feeling of shame. Maybe I have done something silly, I feel ashamed and embarrassed, and I don't want my friends to know, so I lie. And then I lie to cover my lies, and so on. This type of lying is called *saving face*.

3. To get something
One time I told my mom I had done my homework, so she took me to the movies. Well, guess what: I lied. I felt so bad about this that I confessed before we walked into the movie theater. She praised me for telling the truth and forgave me.

4. To be popular among your friends
Everyone wants to be successful and praised. Some people work hard to deserve the praise, and others lie about their achievements to impress their friends.

Why Lying is bad.

Lying is harmful in many ways.

If you lie...

- people will stop trusting you, they won't be friends or work with you

- you can get into trouble with the law

- people will be less able to help you because you gave them wrong information

- other people can get into trouble because of your lie

Why is it so easy to get into trouble when lying? Because lying is much harder than telling the truth. You have to come up with stories that never happened and make sure you remember how you told those stories, because if one time you tell them differently people will notice and know that you are lying. The methods of detecting a lie are all based on the fact that it takes a lot of effort and stress to lie.

How to Detect a Lie: Words a Liar Chooses

When a person is lying, they are trying to convince you that their story is real, so they give you a lot of detail, **more detail than we normally remember.**

They can also use words like *honestly* or *to tell you the truth*. If you are just telling the story why would you start with the word *honestly*?

A lier often **repeats words again and again** such as *I didn't, I didn't*, or they may **repeat a question you asked**, or ask you *Why do you ask that?* rather than answering your question.

They do this to delay answering you, so they have more time to think, and they are **choosing their words much more carefully** than a person who tells the truth.

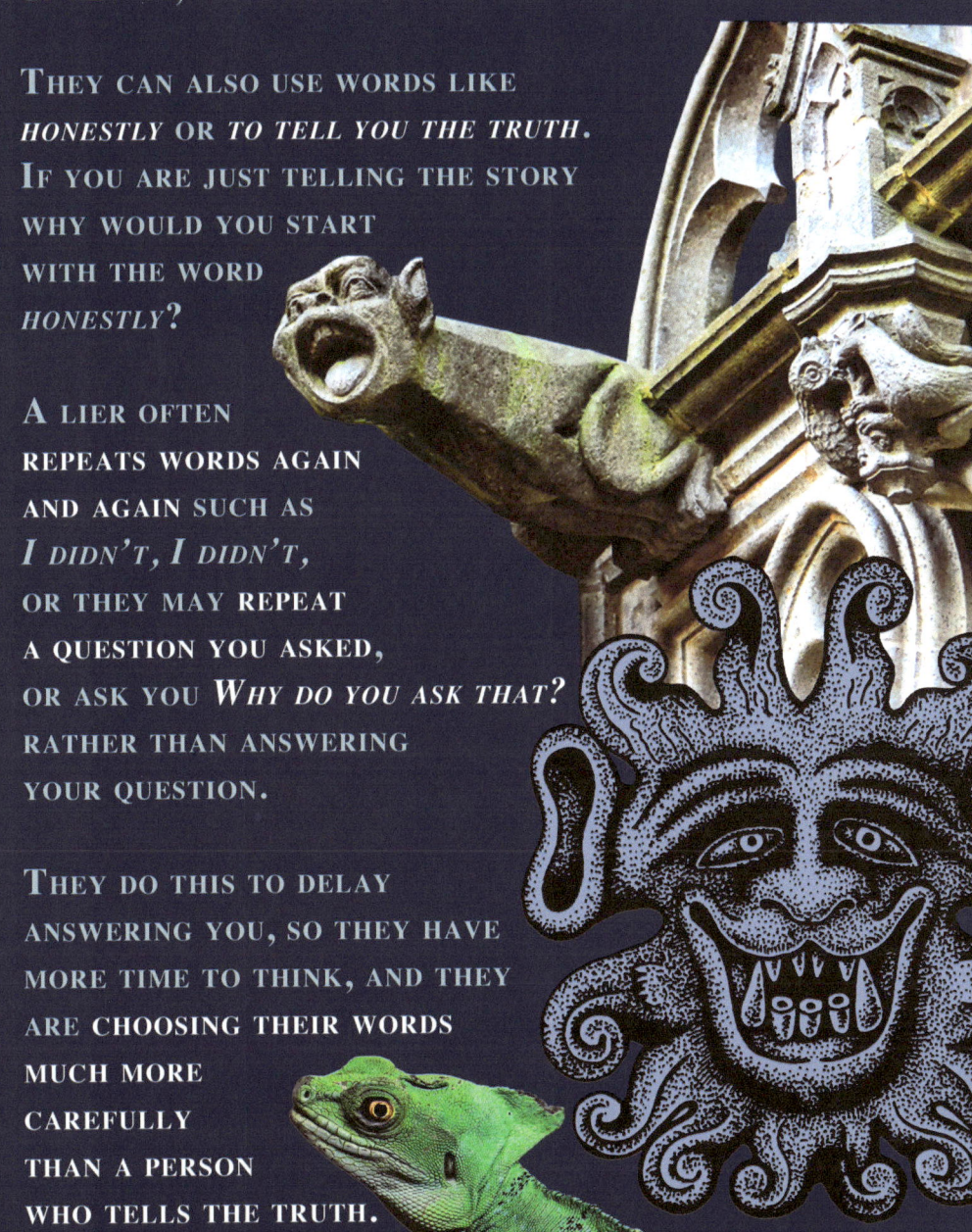

How to Detect a Lie
Body Language (1)

A person's body language can tell you they are lying. Body language is what we say without using words. For example, touching your face, or tilting your head, or crossing your arms are all examples of body language. When a person is lying, they worry that you won't believe them, so their behavior shows signs of anxiety or worrying.

- When someone is lying to you, **watch their eyes**. Often they are **darting back and forth**. Also the person may **look down or away**, trying to avoid looking you in the eye. Another sign of lying is if a person is **staring** you in the eyes without blinking.

- When a person is lying they often feel like **covering their face:** they may put their hands over their mouth, or eyes, or nose.

How to Detect a Lie
Body Language (2)

- **We blink about five or six times a minute, but a person who is lying may blink five or six times in a row**, very fast.

- **If a person closes their eyes for a second or two**, this may also mean that they are lying. It's another way to avoid looking at you.

- **A fake smile** is another sign of lying. When the smile is real, your eyes smile, and the skin around them wrinkles. But if a person smiles only with their mouth, it's a fake smile.

- Because a liar is worrying, their blood rushes to their face and they may **blush or start sweating**.

- Because of this the skin on their face may itch, they will **touch their face**, or rub their forehead, or wipe their nose - these can be signs of lying.

How to Detect a Lie
Body Language (3)

- When you ask a right-handed person about something they saw, they normally look up and to their left (or sometimes straight ahead) to remember what happened. But if they are lying, they would look up and to their right. This is how our eyes move when we use imagination, rather than memory.

Left-handed people will look up and to their right (or straight ahead) to remember things, and up and to their left if they use their imagination.

- When we try to remember what we heard, our eyes move toward our left ear, but if a person's eyes move right, it's likely they are about to lie.

- When we try to remember a smell, a touch, or whether it was cold or hot, our eyes move down and left. But if a person's eyes go down and right, it's possible that they are lying.

How to Detect a Lie
Body Language (4)

- Lying makes your body tense and your mouth dry, so a liar's **lips** are often very tight or pursed.
- A liar's **voice can change,** becoming higher, as if they are out of breath.
- People who are lying often **turn or tilt their head real fast.** So if you've just asked them a question, and notice a sudden movement of their head, this can be a sign of lying.

Liar's **breathing is often heavy or fast,** and their shoulders can rise.

- Sometimes a liar is so nervous, they **will sit very still, hardly moving at all.**

- And sometimes a liar will be **fidgeting** in their chair. This may be the reason they say *Liar, liar, pants on fire!*

How to Detect a Lie
Body Language (5)

- **Lying is stressful. When a person is lying sometimes they try to relax and feel more at ease by rocking, twirling hair around a finger, or playing with a ring, or their clothes.**

They may act like they brush dust off their clothes, or rub their palms on their pant legs. Most people do this from time to time, but when people lie, they do it more.

- **Liars often hunch over, as if they are trying to make themselves smaller, or lean away from you. They can try to hide their hands, or cover the dip between their neck and collar bone with a hand.**

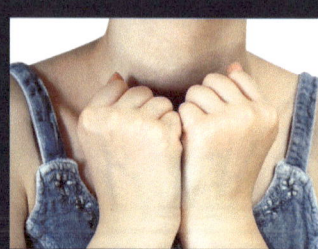

Liar!

How to Detect a Lie
Questions to Ask

You can try to find out if someone is lying to you by asking that person a few questions and watching how they react and respond.

First ask them a couple questions that have nothing to do with what you think they are going to lie about. Ask them about the weather, or what they are planning to do on the weekend.

When they answer, watch their body language and how their eyes move.

Because while answering these simple questions they are probably not lying, you will find out how they look and behave when they are telling the truth.

Next ask them the questions to which you think they will answer with lies. Now watch for changes in body language and word choice.

How to Help Someone Confess

What is it to confess?
To confess means to tell the truth, even if you would rather keep it to yourself.
Sometimes a person is lying because they are afraid of punishment, or afraid that they won't be respected for what they've done.

Very often they will stop lying and confess, if you make them feel comfortable and respected. To help someone tell the truth, you should be calm and talk to them respectfully.

Don't call what they are doing *a lie*. Instead, you can say, *I think you're not telling me the whole truth.* You can also say, *You know you can trust me.*

Show respect by saying *I know you are honest. You can trust me and tell me the truth.* When they hear that you think they are honest, they may want to live up to that, and stop lying.

How to Detect a Lie
Lie Detector (1)

A lie detector, also called a polygraph is a machine that records how fast your heart beats, how fast you breathe, your blood pressure, and whether your skin is sweaty or dry while you answer questions. It was invented in 1921 in the US, and is used by police and private detectives.

The lie detector test lasts for 10 minutes. They put a few sensors (measuring devices) on your fingers or palm, wrap some tubes around your chest and stomach, and put a movement detector on your chair. The sensors and tubes are connected to the lie detector machine.

Next they ask you a few CONTROL QUESTIONS. These are questions like *What is your name? How old are you?* to which you most likely won't lie. They record your breathing, pulse and so on, as you answer these questions.

Now they know how your body reacts when you tell the truth.

Polygraph test

How to Detect a Lie
Lie Detector (2)

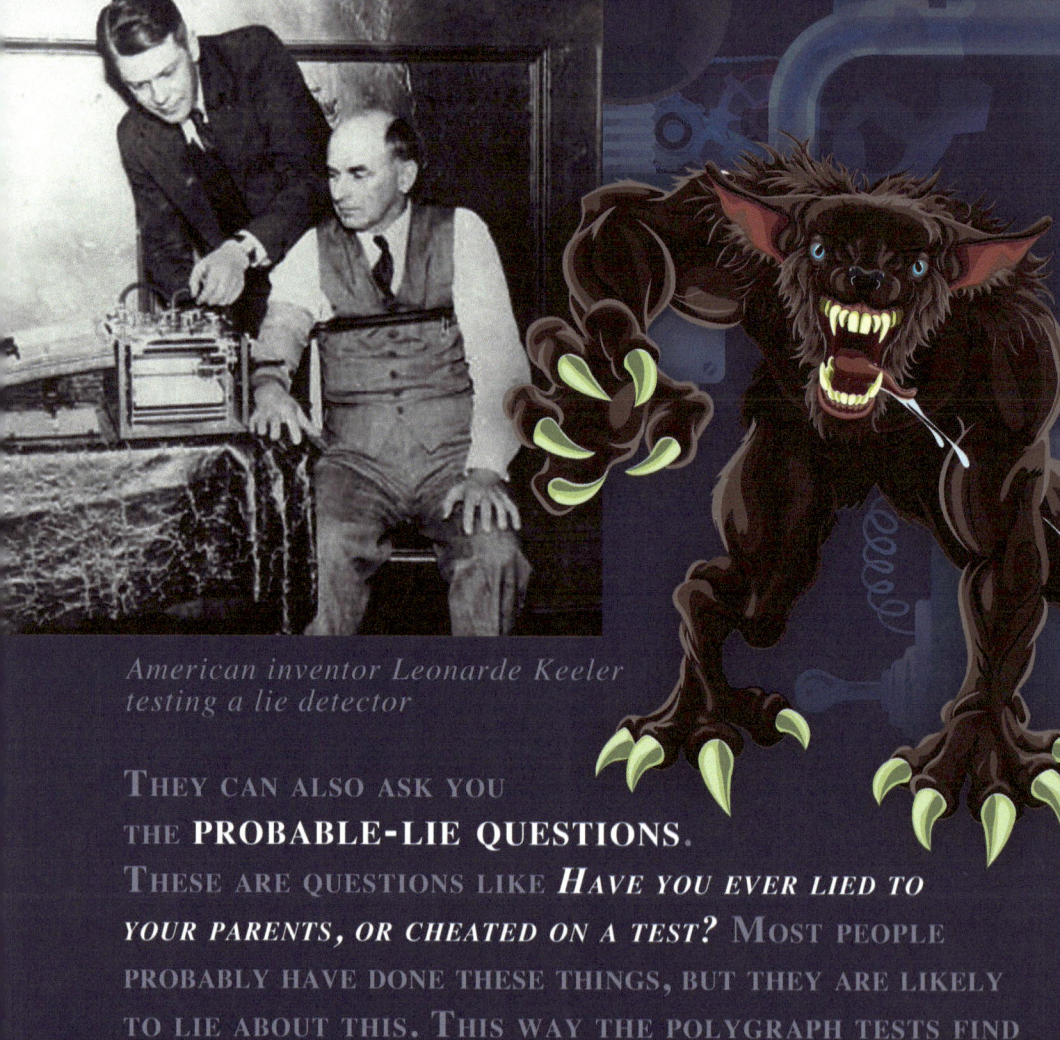

American inventor Leonarde Keeler testing a lie detector

They can also ask you the **PROBABLE-LIE QUESTIONS**. These are questions like *Have you ever lied to your parents, or cheated on a test?* Most people probably have done these things, but they are likely to lie about this. This way the polygraph tests find out **how you behave when you are lying**.

Next they ask you the actual **LIE-DETECTING QUETIONS**. Again, they record how your body reacts and compare it with your reaction to the control and probable-lie questions.

How Good are Lie Detectors?

Unfortunately, not great. The problem is the **polygraph machine records only how nervous you are** when you answer questions. But being nervous doesn't always mean you are lying. For example, **you can just be stressed out**, or afraid of the lie detector test, and the machine records that you are nervous. As a result, sometimes honest answers look like a lie. This is called a **false positive**. The lie detector says yes, the person is lying, but actually they are honest! They say that if the test is conducted really well, it will be accurate in **8 questions out of 10**. Some experts, however, believe it's only **6 out of 10**, and that's not good at all. **You can toss a coin and get the same result!**

When police investigate a crime, they use lie detectors, but in the **US** courts judges almost never allow the results of a lie detector test to be used in deciding whether a person is guilty or not.

Can You Beat a Lie Detector Test?

Yes, but you may need training to do this, the kind of training spies get. **Here is how spies cheat on the polygraph test.**

Because the test compares results recorded during control questions with the results recorded during the lie-detecting questions, the spies pretend they are 1. nervous during control questions and 2. super confident and relaxed during the lie-detecting questions. This way the machine records truth as lie, and lie as truth.

How can you pretend you are nervous? You can bite your tongue, or step on a thumbtack hidden in your shoe. The pain will make you sweat and breathe faster, and the polygraph machine will record it as being nervous, or lying.

How can you be super calm during lie-detecting questions? Some spies say they imagine being on the beach, or at a party with friends. They feel instantly relaxed and trick the machine.

Spies also try to be **super friendly with the person who asks them questions**, because this person interprets the results of the test, and if they see you relaxed, friendly, joking and laughing, they are more likely to also see you as honest.

PINOCCHIO

Pinocchio and his father Gepetto

When a lier is nervous and touching their nose, it's known as *the Pinocchio effect*.

Pinocchio is a wooden toy shaped like a boy from the novel *Pinocchio* by Italian author Carlo Collodi.

Pinocchio was selfish and often lied, and every time he lied his nose would grow longer and longer!

It took him a long time to learn to be honest, and when he did, he changed from a wooden toy into a real boy.

Can Animals Lie?

Think animals are nice honest citizens of the animal kingdom? You are in for a shock! Wait till you hear this!...

Liar!

Blue Jay

Hawk

Blue Jays

Blue Jays can imitate the calls of hawks. So a blue jay hides in the bushes near a bird feeder, and starts making hawk sounds. Birds at the bird feeder think a hawk is attacking and run for their lives (sorry, fly for their lives) from the bird feeder, leaving all the food to the blue jay! And blue jays get away with this again and again! The good news is this doesn't work with people. I am sure you have heard this story:

The Boy Who Cried *Wolf!*

So this boy was guarding sheep in the field, and he decided to scare people as a joke, and started screaming *Wolf!* People from the village came running to save the boy, but there was no wolf. The boy thought it was funny and did it again. Then, one day, a real wolf showed up. The boy cried *Wolf!* But people thought it was a joke and didn't come...

Cuckoo

Ok, so you think blue jays are bad...Wait till you hear what cuckoos do! Cuckoos sneak their eggs into other birds' nests, and those birds raise little cuckoos thinking they are their own kids! Now this is a real crime! Cuckoos should be behind bars, not flying around going *cu-ckoo*! They are **criminals and bad parents**!

Squirrels Are Nutcases!

Squirrels trick other squirrels! They pretend to bury a nut in the ground, but actually they hide it in their cheek, move to the next place and start digging again. They repeat this a few times, so if a squirrel thief is watching them, the bad squirrel never knows for sure where the nut is hidden!

White Lies

Liar liar feathers on fire!

Blue jays, cuckoos and squirrels are such experienced liars, they could probably beat a polygraph test!

However, there are some situations in the bird world, when **birds lie to save their family**. These are white lies, and the birds that do this usually have a nest on the ground, where a predator, like a cat, can find it.

When a bird notices a predator near its nest, it pretends that its wing is broken. It hops on the ground flapping one wing and dragging the other wing, slowly fluttering away from the nest. The cat follows it, getting ready to pounce. But when they are far enough from the nest, the clever bird just flies away. **The Killdeer** is the best at this broken wing act. By the way, it got it's name from its call. It sounds like *kill-deer kill-deer!*

killdeer pretending its wing is broken

Why Kids Lie

Not only animals lie. Sometimes kids lie too. Why? Experts say **preschool kids** don't yet understand the difference between truth and lie. They make up stories just for fun. These lies can simply mean that the kid is creative.

Schoolkids lie to cover their mistakes, because they are afraid to disappoint their parents or teachers. If the grownup finds out and doesn't get mad, the kid may confess and apologize. If this happens to you, remember: you want grownups to trust you. If they trust you, they will allow you more things, and if you make a mistake, they won't be angry. Trust is like wings. When you can fly, you don't have to hide and lie!

Older schoolkids and teenagers may lie to avoid telling their parents about their school life or friends simply because they want to be independent. Is this a good reason to lie? No. It will only make their parents worry more, and demand answers. Much better to be honest, and explain to your parents that it's time to treat you more like a grownup.

Is Pretend Play a Lie?

No. Some very little kids like to pretend they have a pet. They play with it, and take it for a walk. It's an imaginary pet. When a kid is talking about it, it's play, not a lie.

Also when kids are little they like to believe in magical creatures, like Santa Claus or the Tooth Fairy. Parents often play along and tell kids the Christmas gifts they bought are from Santa, and the candy under their pillow is from the Tooth Fairy. Are parents lying?
No, it's pretend play, same as an imaginary pet.

If you know a little kid who believes in Santa, you are not going to upset them by telling them Santa is not real, right? They will guess it on their own one day, just like you did.

Older kids like to pretend they are a character from their favorite movie or book. And it's so great for you, because in this play you use your imagination and learn to handle different situations, to talk about your feelings, to explain and defend your ideas.

Better Avoid these!

There are some lies most kids say, and all parents know about. Some of these are not really lies becuase you think this is true when you are saying this. But your parents probably won't believe you. Just warning!...

- If we get a dog, I promise I'll take care of it!
- I swear I won't ask for anything again after this.
- I think I'm too sick to go to school today.
- Of course I ate the lunch you packed.
- Dad said I could.
- I forgot.
- The teacher didn't give us homework.
- I'll do it tomorrow.
- But everyone else failed, too!
- My friends' parents allow this!
- He started it!

I fibbed here and there as a kid, and at some point I realized lying is just too stressful and not worth it. I also want to give you this advice... Some kids like to look smart, and they will bliff to pretend they know more than they actually know. And then there are kids who pretend they can't do homework because it's too hard, or because they don't know enough, but actually they are just tired or maybe a bit lazy at that moment...

Well, please remember, that if you have to lie, it's **always better to pretend that you are smart, rather than that you are stupid.** Don't say *I can't*. Say the truth: *I am tired, bored, and I need to take a break.*

What is Your Conscience?

Your conscience is a feeling or voice inside your mind that tells you whether your behavior is right or wrong. Your conscience is your understanding of what is right and what is wrong. For example, you may do something that hurts another person, and you instantly know what you've done is wrong. We call this the voice of your conscience, but actually it's your own voice, because you know that hurting others is wrong.

Your conscience is stricter than the law. The law doesn't say you can't insult another person, but your conscience tells you it's bad. Some things are legal (not forbidden by the law), but they are still not right. The law doesn't tell you to help a person in trouble, but your conscience tells you you should.

LIES IN ADVERTISEMENT

Advertisements (or ads) give information about products in order to sell them. Whenever you see ads, watch out: They often bend the truth!

For example, here is an ad promising that if you take these pills, you will lose weight. Well, one thing this ad doesn't say is that to lose weight you also need to eat only this, and do this every day!!!

This type of lie is called *Lying by Omission*. *Omission* means *not saying something, omitting it*. This ad also uses **exaggeration**: It doesn't say *some weight*, but *a lot of weight*. Kids' TV shows play a lot of ads making kids want toys. But when parents buy that shiny toy, kids often realize they didn't want that toy at all. An ad talked them into it!

Con Artists (1)

A con artist is a person who cheats others by making them believe something that is not true in order to make them pay money to the con artist.

Con stands for confidence. Con artists first make people trust them (gaining their confidence), but then deceive them.

In 1905 French con artist Henri Lemoine convinced the diamond mining and jewelry company De Beers that he had invented a way to make diamonds from coal. They paid him a lot of money to keep his invention secret and to sell it to them. Then, in 1908 a jeweler in Paris revealed that instead of making diamonds Lemoine was buying them from his shop!

American con artist William Elmer Mead made friends with a wealthy builder. One day when they were togehter, they saw a man drop a wallet full of money. They returned the wallet to him and he took them out to dinner as a thank you. The wallet owner was Mead's helper. He pretended he owned sports stadiums, and offered to rent them to the builder, so he could sell tickets for people to watch the Halley's Comet that was coming near Earth in 1910. The builder agreed and wrote the two con artists a check for the rent.

CON ARTISTS (2)

VICTOR LUSTIG pretended he worked for the French government, and that France wanted to sell the famous Eiffel Tower in Paris. The tower is made from iron, so he found people who bought and sold iron, and invited them to a secret meeting. One of them paid Lustig a huge sum of money for the tower. Then Lustig invited another group of iron buyers, and sold the Eiffel Tower a second time!!

GEORGE C. PARKER was an American con artist who did the same con trick as Victor Lustig, selling the Brooklyn Bridge in New York City. He convinced his victims that they could collect money from people crossing the bridge. He also pretended to sell the Statue of Liberty!

An Oath

Before you testify, or give testimony in court (testifying, or testimony is saying what you know about a crime, or court case), you have to take an oath, which means you promise to tell the truth. In the US they usually tell you:
Please raise your right hand to take the oath...
Do you solemnly swear that you will tell the truth, the whole truth, and nothing but the truth?
You raise your right hand and say yes.
In many courts you say the oath with your right hand raised and your left hand on the Bible.

Why do we raise our right hand when taking an oath in court? In 17th century England crimes were punished by branding a person's right hand. Branding is using a super hot stamp to burn a letter or any other sign onto one's skin. So raising your right hand you showed the court that you had never been convicted of a crime.

Perjury

If you took an oath promising to tell the truth, and broke your promise, it's called perjury. The word perjury comes from 2 Latin words: *per* (through) and *jurare* (to swear) Lying under oath is a crime.
In the US a person who lies under oath will have to pay a big fine (a fine is money you pay as a punishment for a crime) or go to prison.

The Fifth Amendment

The Fifth Amendment (an amendment is a change, or addition) to the United States Constitution is part of the United States Law. It says that you don't have to give any information that will help prove that you have committed a crime. So criminals *take the fifth*, which means they don't have to take an oath in court and tell the truth about their own crimes. Sometimes even people who saw a crime happen, or know something about it (witnesses) take the fifth if they are not sure they remember everything correctly, or are afraid to make a false statement under oath.

INTERROGATION

The 6th Amendment to the US Constitution says that any person accused of a crime is **innocent** (innocent = not guilty) **until proven guilty.** This means that if a criminal is lying and doesn't admit to his crime, the police have to prove he did it.

The police conduct a criminal investigation to find out the truth. They look for **witnesses**, and collect the **evidence** (things that show who committed the crime, like finger prints, or security camera video).

They also **interrogate** the **suspect**. They can't call him a criminal until they prove he did it, and until the court decides he is guilty of the crime. **Interrogation** is a conversation between the police and the suspect, where the police try to separate truth from lies. There are a few interrogation methods. The best known is the **good cop - bad cop,** when one police investigator pretends he is angry and threatens the suspect, and the other one pretends he is friendly, so that the suspect tells him the truth.

MIRANDA RIGHTS

BEFORE THE POLICE INTERROGATE A SUSPECT THEY READ HIM A DOCUMENT CALLED THE **MIRANDA WARNING:** *YOU HAVE THE RIGHT TO REMAIN SILENT. ANYTHING YOU SAY WILL BE USED AGAINST YOU IN A COURT OF LAW. YOU HAVE THE RIGHT TO HAVE AN ATTORNEY. IF YOU CANNOT AFFORD ONE, ONE WILL BE APPOINTED TO YOU BY THE COURT. WITH THESE RIGHTS IN MIND, ARE YOU STILL WILLING TO TALK WITH ME ABOUT THE CHARGES AGAINST YOU?*

AN ATTORNEY IS A LAWYER WHO WILL DEFEND THE SUSPECT IN COURT. **CHARGES** ARE WHAT THE SUSPECT IS ACCUSED OF. SO THE SUSPECT CAN USE HIS **FIFTH AMMENDMENT** RIGHT TO SILENCE AND REFUSE TO ANSWER ANY QUESTIONS. IT'S NOT EASY TO GET THE SUSPECT TO CONFESS!

www.ingramcontent.com/pod-product-compliance
Lightning Source LLC
Chambersburg PA
CBHW041506010526
44118CB00001B/32